GIRLS' GUIDES

CRUSHES, CREEPS, AND CLASSMATES

A Girl's Guide to Getting Along with Boys

Elizabeth Frankenberger

the rosen publishing group's

rosen central

new york

Published in 1999 by The Rosen Publishing Group, Inc.
29 East 21st Street, New York, NY 10010

Library of Congress Cataloging-in-Publication Data

Frankenberger, Elizabeth.
    Crushes, creeps, and classmates : a girl's guide to getting along with boys / by Elizabeth Frankenberger.
        p.   cm.
    Includes bibliographical references and index.
    Summary: Outlines some of the differences between boys and girls, including physical and behavioral, and gives adolescent girls advice about boy-girl relationships.
    ISBN 0-8239-2980-9
    1. Teenage boys—Psychology Juvenile literature. 2. Teenage girls—Psychology Juvenile literature. 3. Interpersonal relations in adolescence Juvenile literature. 4. Sex differences (Psychology) Juvenile literature. [1. Teenage boys. 2. Teenage girls. 3. Interpersonal relations. 4. Sex differences.} I. Title.
HQ797.F72 1999
305.235—dc21   99-324403
                                                                                    CIP

Manufactured in the United States of America

$\textbf{C}$ontents

About This Book

The middle school years are like a roller coaster—wild and scary but also fun and way cool. One minute you're way, way up there, and the next minute you're plunging down into the depths. Not surprisingly, sometimes you may find yourself feeling confused and lost. Not to worry, though. Just like on a roller-coaster ride, at the end of all this crazy middle school stuff, you'll be laughing and screaming and talking about how awesome it all was.

Right now, however, chances are your body is changing so much that it's barely recognizable, your old friends may not share your interests anymore, and your life at school is suddenly hugely complicated. And let's not even get into the whole boy issue. It's a wonder that you can still think straight at all.

Fortunately, reader dear, help is here. This book is your road map. It's also a treasure chest filled with ideas and advice. Armed with this book and with your own inner strength (trust us, you have plenty), you can safely, confidently navigate the twists and turns of your middle school years. It will be tough going, and sometimes you'll wonder if you'll ever get through it. But you—fabulous, powerful, unique you—are up to the task. This book is just a place to start.

Maxi Pads to Mathematics: Boys and Girls Are Different

1

Sugar and spice and everything nice. Is that still what girls are made of?

Not!

A girl is made up of a lot of ingredients, not all of them sweet. The "cookie-cutter" girl is a thing of the past; she was put back into the drawer years ago with the rest of her mother's old utensils. Today's girl looks much more like Buffy the Vampire Slayer than Cindy Brady. This is not to suggest that teenagers will spend most of their time chasing bloodsuckers! But they may very well find themselves searching for open hearts—specifically those belonging to boys.

Would you ever dream of wearing your hair in bottle curls?!

If you are somewhere between the ages of nine and eighteen, chances are you know a boy who fits into one of these three categories: crushes, classmates, or creeps. You may even know a boy who fits into all three. It's how you choose to deal with these "types" that makes getting along with boys possible.

Us and Them

Most girls are raised to see boys as different from them. Even more important, most girls are raised differently than are boys. The outward signs are often obvious (though not always): Baby boys are dressed in blue, girls in pink; boys often get cropped haircuts, whereas girls wear long ponytails with ribbons or sparkly barrettes; as teenagers boys may prefer to wear hats and sneakers, but teenage girls opt for nail polish and jewelry.

Do you have a brother at home? What types of toys did your brother play with as a child? Were they different from your own? How? How does your brother spend his free

time? What do you do with yours? Was your brother encouraged to play sports, whereas you were directed toward learning to play a musical instrument?

All right, maybe you don't have a brother. Maybe you have a sister, or more than one. Maybe you are an only child. It really doesn't matter. Whether you are white, Latina, African American, Jewish, Buddhist, rich, poor, or whatever, you get the point.

It doesn't matter where you come from or where you go. If you are a girl, you are bound to have noticed that the way boys act, in general, is different from the way girls act. And sometimes, so are the ways in which they are treated at home or at school. If you are honest with yourself, you may have to admit that you do some of these things yourself. Do you think of a girl who likes to build tree forts and loves to play basketball and soccer as a tomboy? Is a boy who likes stuffed animals a "sissy"?

"Stop acting like such a girl," one boy teases another. "That's such a guy thing," your girlfriend complains. Next time you hear something like this, it might be interesting to think about what is really being said.

For example, if boys and girls behave differently, how much is it because they are different, and how much is it because they are expected to act differently? Statistics can be used to imply that there are specifically "male" professions, hobbies, even emotions. For instance, only 15 percent of the scientists and engineers in the United States are women. And in general, throughout junior high and high school, girls tend to do less well in math and science than boys.

So does this mean that boys are naturally better at math and science than girls? Think again. Girls Incorporated, a national research and advocacy group, conducted a study that showed that after elementary school, teachers expect that girls won't perform as well as their male classmates in math and science. Could it be, then, that the different level of performance is the result of different expectations?

These different expectations can affect what we aspire to ourselves. Any boy or girl who watches professional or college basketball knows that playing ball is no longer just a "guy thing." Yet a recent survey of inner-city teenage girls found that their greatest pastime is sitting around watching the *boys* shoot hoops.

What's the 411?

Okay, the point of this book is not to highlight all the many differences between the genders to make you think of boys and girls as existing on separate islands far away from each other. After all, these differences are a large part of what makes boys and girls so interested in each other. But let's face it: Fitting boys into your daily life can be difficult.

There's the one who steals your heart like Leonardo DiCaprio. There's every girl's worst nightmare: the Big, Bad Bully. And then there's the rest of the gang—skateboarding around the school yard, belching in the cafeteria, throwing paper airplanes in the classroom, and standing by the punch bowl at the school dance.

➤ "The guy I like thinks my best friend is the prettiest girl in the class," Shartryce complains.

➤ "As a joke, a boy grabbed my back to see if I was wearing a bra," Germania recalls. "But I sure didn't think it was funny."

➤ "The boys at my school are interested only in sports or playing video games," Lorre says. "How dull!"

Yeah, boys sure are different. Is this how it will always be? In some ways, maybe. But as this Girl's Guide will show you, there are ways you can understand these differences—and even come to appreciate and enjoy them.

Our Bodies, Ourselves: Adolescence and the Female

2

Margaret and Menstruation

One of the most famous adolescents in literature is Margaret Simon, the twelve-year-old heroine of Judy Blume's *Are You There God? It's Me, Margaret.* The thing Margaret wants more than anything else is to get her period. Why? Because it means she's finally growing up and changing from a little girl to a woman.

When a girl gets her period—or in medical terms, begins the cycle of menstruation—it means that her reproductive organs have reached maturity. From about age ten to twenty, a girl's body transforms dramatically, even more so than a boy's. What this means in junior high school, for

Girls often have their own, special language. "Aunt Dot" is one such example. Who's that? Well, your period, of course! There are hundreds of ways to refer to the period during which you menstruate. "On the rag," "Red light," "See Spot run," "Girl rush," and certainly others. One of the nicest things about being a girl is sharing your experiences with other girls. Girls know what it's like being girls, thank goodness!

instance, is that you might hear a boy's voice crack now and then. Meanwhile, you have already started to wear deodorant and a bra. You may even have started getting your period.

Christine sometimes worries that she doesn't seem to be growing up as quickly as her classmates. "Will I have to wait forever?" she worries. "I have a bra, but I don't have anything to put in it!"

Wendy worries that maybe she is growing too fast. "My thighs are expanding," she thinks as she looks in the mirror. "Am I going to be fat when I grow up?"

Every girl goes through the same physical/chemical changes, but not necessarily at the same age or pace. Some girls may develop bigger hips or smaller breasts or grow more or less quickly than their classmates. Puberty can be divided into roughly five stages. The phases may overlap, but here is a set of basic guidelines:

Stage One (eight to eleven)

On the outside of your body, things look normal. But inside, you've got it going on! Your brain has stimulated the release of hormones that you'll need later for menstrual and childbearing functions.

Stage Two (eleven to fourteen)

Welcome, breasts! Early pubic hairs begin to surface. You have probably grown some inches— in height or on your thighs, both of which are normal and healthy.

Stage Three (nine to fifteen)

Your hormones continue to produce changes inside and outside of your body. There is also an increase in ovary development.

Stage Four (ten to sixteen)

Fuller breasts, coarser pubic hair, a pimple or two. Or three. Sweat glands are in full-force (hint: deodorant). Your ovaries are producing eggs. When the time is right, a ripe egg will be released. This is the first step in a girl's menstrual cycle.

Stage Five (twelve to nineteen)

Adios to puberty. Your breasts have reached their full size, your pubic hair is all there, and you've pretty much stopped growing. If you have not already started your period, it should begin during this stage.

At these ages, a boy's body is changing too. While you are producing eggs, he is beginning to produce sperm. Outwardly, his physical changes may not be as noticeable as yours—yet.

Mirror, Mirror, on the Wall

3

So your body is starting to look different to you. It also looks different to boys. This is why the sexes generally do not share the same bathrooms and gym lockers! Generally boys mature less rapidly than girls. What this often means is that they, in fact, have an even harder time than girls in adjusting to the changes they are going through. They may not be physically ready for s-e-x, but they are no doubt curious about it. They have been looking at television, magazines, photos, and movies, and they've got some idea of what a developed girl looks like. Inevitably they will begin to examine girls' bodies with greater curiosity than ever before. You might be noticing this and feeling a little (or a lot) self-conscious around boys.

But let's go back to the big question: "Who's the fairest of them all?"

It's natural to wonder what other people think of your appearance. Such concerns increase during adolescence. But sometimes things get twisted around: Girls, who are also looking at images of women on television and in magazines, begin to look at themselves from the outside in, basing their worth on the way they look in the mirror.

"I can't possibly go to school with a pimple on my chin!" Yamaleth fumes.

"No wonder he doesn't like me. Look at how wide my hips are!" Kelly obsesses.

Newsflash:

All teenagers go through that charming "awkward physical stage"—not to mention a range of chaotic emotions. As if your body's constant changing wasn't enough of a ride, the hormones surging through you have another fabulous side effect: emotional intensity (like rocketing from ecstatic to miserable in the blink of an eye). If possible, try to keep this in mind next time you find yourself on the verge of a major freak-out. When you hit puberty, being a total weirdo is totally normal.

It can be hard to appreciate yourself at such a turbulent time in your life. Our society tells young women that they are supposed to look beautiful, be thin, chase boys, and do "girl" things. With images of models and movie stars every-where, it's easy to see why many teenage girls think they fall short in the appearance department. And with images of the female body used to sell every-thing from cars to cell phones to candy bars, it's easy to see why we sometimes feel like objects around members of the opposite sex.

FACT:
More than 40 million American women wear a size 14 or larger.

So does everything boil down to the way we look on the outside? It might seem that way sometimes. The "pretty" girls get asked to dance; the rest sit out. Still, the answer is no. Appearance is not the end of the story.

What makes a girl attractive is much more than the way she looks. It is her individual talents, her ability to make friends, the music she likes to listen to, the books she likes to read, the sports she excels in, and much, much more. In short, what makes a girl attractive is what makes her, her.

Let's Talk About Sex

Vagina.
  Okay? You can take a deep breath now or have a laugh. The word will not be used again in this book!
  Phew!
  Why is it that names of certain body parts—sexual organs, especially—sometimes strike us as funny? One reason may be that they make us a little nervous, and laughing is a way to relieve tension. First of all, as young children we may not know the real words for certain parts of our bodies but use funny nicknames instead. Young people often are not explicitly told what "sex" means, and in fact many kids are discouraged from learning about it. Hopefully, at some point our parents or teachers will give us "the birds and the bees, 101." But all too often, issues about sex are dealt with in very quiet, even untruthful ways.

So how is a girl supposed to know what to do about sex, anyway?

Well, the most important thing a girl can do is get the facts. *Puhleese*, do not make any decisions regarding sex until you know the whole story. That means knowing how your body works, how to prevent pregnancy and STDs, how to say NO when you're not comfortable, and how to keep yourself safe at all times and in all situations.

Once you have the facts, you may or may not be eager to answer the question for yourself: Am I ready to have sex?

There is no one answer to this question. Girls answer it in a variety of ways:

> "I've kissed a boy, but I'm not having sex until I'm eighteen," is how Virginia Marie has chosen to deal with this question.

> "I'm twelve, and I've been to third base," is how Allison characterizes her sexual experience.

> "My boyfriend is a few years older than I am. He's ready to have sex," Catherine confides to a friend.

> "I don't know when I'll be ready to have sex. I've never been in love," Sara thinks.

> "I don't find boys' bodies especially attractive. I may never have sex," is the way Chelsea feels right now.

> "I'm starting to be interested in boys, but the physical stuff can wait. There's plenty of time for that," Taisha believes.

> "Sex is for marriage," is the way Faith was brought up.

What are your parents' attitudes about sex? Do they ever talk about it with you, or is it a forbidden topic in your household? How is sex viewed or discussed in school? Do your friends talk about it a lot, if at all?

There is definitely a lot to learn, so let's use this pop quiz to find out how much you know already.

Questions

1. If I don't have my period by age ____, I must not be developing properly.
a. 12   b. 14   c. 16   d. none of the above.

2. Masturbation is . . .
a. a natural way of exploring your own body.   b. illegal in some states.   c. something that girls do if they don't have boyfriends.
d. none of the above.

3. Sexual intercourse is . . .
a. the way two people express their love for each other.   b. dangerous under the age of eighteen.   c. shameful unless you're married.   d. none of the above.

4. Homosexuality is . . .
a. what causes AIDS.   b. an unnatural means of expressing love or sexual desire.   c. both (a) and (b).   d. none of the above.

5. I can become pregnant if I . . .
a. have sexual intercourse.   b. have sexual intercourse without using contraception.
c. have sexual intercourse and use contraception.   d. all of the above.

The Answers:

1. None of the above. Girls' bodies mature at different rates. There is no "right" age at which a girl begins her menstrual cycle. The average age, however, is around fourteen.

2. Masturbation is a natural way of exploring your own body. Despite what some people may think, it is nothing to be ashamed of.

3. None of the above. Yes, some people have intercourse as a way of expressing their love for each other, but this is not the exclusive definition. Sex means different things to different people. Some people believe that it is wrong to have sex before marriage and view sex only as a means of having children.

4. None of the above. A homosexual is a person who has sexual desire for a person of the same sex as him- or herself. There is nothing wrong with having such feelings, though some people do believe that homosexuality is "unnatural" or immoral. You cannot get AIDS just by being a homosexual.

5. All of the above. The only guaranteed way to prevent pregnancy is not to have sexual intercourse. Contraceptives do greatly reduce the risk of pregnancy, but none of them work each and every time. Certain kinds of contraceptives, such as condoms, also reduce the risk of sexually transmitted diseases (STDs).

Like it or not, when you think about sex, you have to think about STDs. You should know the names of STDs—HIV/AIDS, gonorrhea, syphilis, herpes, chlamydia, and HPV (human papilloma virus)—and you should know their symptoms. You should know that in women, some of these diseases, especially chlamydia, show no symptoms. You should know that some of them (AIDS, gonorrhea, and syphilis, for example) can be fatal. You should know that some of the others (such as herpes and HPV) are incurable. You must know that all of them require immediate medical attention and can have severe long-term health consequences, including negative effects on your ability to have children.

You need to know that you can get an STD from having sexual intercourse just once, with just one boy, just as you can get pregnant from just one act of intercourse—even if it's the first and only time. Finally, and most important, you need to know that if you decide to have sex, you should ALWAYS use a condom.

Stat Chat

The average age at which teens become sexually active in this country is fifteen.

Each year, four million adolescents in the United States contract STDS.

In a single act of unprotected sex, a woman has a 50 percent chance of getting gonorrhea and a 30 percent chance of getting herpes.

The rate of infection from the most deadly of these diseases, HIV/AIDS, is highest among young, straight women between the ages of thirteen and nineteen.

Yet in a recent survey, almost 70 percent of adolescents "radically underestimate" the prevalence of STDS.

You are approaching the age where, like it or not, you'll need to make a lot of decisions about yourself, your body, your behavior, and sex. And the time to start thinking is, as always, *before* you act. To make wise decisions, you need to get as much information as you can. If you want to learn more or are afraid you might be at risk for having an STD, talk to your family doctor or contact one of the organizations listed in the It's a Girl's World section at the back of the book.

Crushes: He Loves Me, He Loves Me Not . . .

5

Have you ever picked petals off of a daisy, aching for a "he loves me" at the stem? Do the butterflies in your stomach feel a bit more like, say, peacocks? Do your palms sweat before English class, or do you daydream during social studies?

Then you have been there.

The word "crush" implies a kind of falling: heavy matter, deep emotions. Sometimes a crush feels great, like a shot of rocket fuel. Other times it can cause you to feel sluggish, sad, and hopeless—especially if your crush does not feel the same about you, or worse yet, doesn't even know you exist.

Crushes come in all shapes and sizes. You could have a crush that lasts the five minutes it takes you to walk to your locker from social studies class, and it could be over by the time you stroll into math. But your next crush could last for months and go from feeling like the most exciting thing ever to some kind of bad rash that you can't find a cure for.

And what if (God forbid!) your best gal pal leaks the secret identity of your crush to her science partner, and suddenly the info is public knowledge? In other words: HE KNOWS!

Well, boys are mysterious. If a guy finds out

he's the object of your crush, he might ask you to go CD shopping after school one day, and then might laugh and totally ignore you the next. To make things more confusing, just because he laughs doesn't necessarily mean that he doesn't like you. He may be embarrassed or confused by his own feelings.

You might even find yourself with a crush on a girl. Girl crushes are a normal part of growing up. They have as much to do with your natural curiosity about being a woman as they do with your sexual orientation.

Could It Be Love?

Adults sometimes feel that because young people are undergoing so many physical and emotional changes, their emotions are somehow not quite "real," in an "oh, you'll get over it" kind of way. Nevertheless, your feelings are valid—even if people tell you otherwise. A fourteen-year-old girl can fall just as deeply in love as a woman in her late twenties. Whether she is ready or able to deal with all the potential consequences of that love is another question. Here, several young women talk about their "crushing" experiences:

Annah

"I will never forget my first love," remembers Annah. "His name was Danny, and we used to talk on the phone for hours at a time. He'd play his guitar for me; I'd read him the lyrics to my favorite songs. I thought he liked me. I thought I loved him. One night he asked me if my best friend, Liza, would ever go out with him. I was his buddy, he told me. But he wanted Liza to be his girlfriend. Soon they started going out. I was devastated and lost all my motivation to do schoolwork, even to eat. That was fifteen years ago, when I was thirteen, and I can still remember every detail."

Maya

"The first time I had sex, I was sixteen," remembers Maya, a college student. "It was during the summer, and his parents were away for the weekend. I told my mom that I was sleeping over at a friend's house. I felt guilty, but he had the best evening planned: a burger barbecue and swimming at his neighbor's pool. That was one of the most fun, romantic nights of my entire life."

Tanya

Tanya, who is now thirty-five, remembers that "I had the biggest crush on my friend's sister, Suzy. She was seventeen, and she had long red hair. I used to go over to their house after school. Once, she showed me her extensive nail polish collection, which she kept under her bed. I remember my heart was pounding so hard, I was sure she could hear it."

All girls have a crush story. The thing to remember is that life is a long series of experiences and experiments—some productive, some failed. And even the so-called failures are things we learn from. That guy who is breaking your heart right now may not be important to you in seven months. Or seven days.

Creeps

A lot of boys are rambling around out there, and let's face it, some boys are bound to act like creeps. Chances are you know exactly who we're talking about: the guy who spits loogies dangerously near you in the hall, the guy who knocks your books out of your hands, the guy who makes "woof woof" noises when you walk by. And oh, the list goes on and on. It seems as though there's one bra-strap snapper in practically every gaggle of guys.

Of course, girls tease and giggle and do mean things too. That can be pretty bad news, but for now, let's just focus on the boy-related dramas and traumas of middle school.

Creeps are a fact of life. Just as you count on the sun coming up in the morning, you can trust that most boys will behave badly toward girls at some point.

Remember what we said earlier about boys being more curious about girls' bodies than before? Well, unfortunately, sometimes that curiosity takes the shape of teasing. And that teasing can take the shape of some pretty mean things being said about parts of your changing body you'd just as soon no one ever thought about.

How do you possibly deal with these rude comments? Well, there's strength in numbers. Don't take it alone: Get your girlfriends together and talk about your feelings. Chances are they've got some similar tales of woe. If you keep the hurt and frustration inside, you'll probably carry around those insults in your head for a lot longer than if you just let yourself vent about it for a minute (or an hour).

Laugh at them. They're so insecure, they'll think they said something stupid. Then they'll stop.
—Tess, age fifteen

Of course, with some creeps what you see is what you get, and they don't ever seem to change. There will be times when you can't just shrug off a guy as being a jerk and get on with your day. If you find that a boy in your life is being more than just your average, run-of-the-mill creep and is actually scaring you or harassing you, make sure you know your rights. The bottom line: Harassment is not okay, and you don't have to put up with it.

Hopefully your school has a harassment policy already established and is prepared to help you deal with this kind of situation. Start by looking at your copy of the school rules that you got at the beginning of the year. If your school doesn't have any specific rules in place yet, it needs some. Get the ball rolling! You'll be helping yourself get through your own experience, and you'll help future students too.

Talk to a teacher, a school counselor, your parents, your coach, or your gorilla-sized older brother, and let them know what's going on. There's an old saying that boys will be boys.

That may be true to some degree, but it's no excuse to deny you your safety and comfort.

So how do you learn to swim with the sharks? The important thing to remember is not to let a creep  affect the way you think of yourself. No boy is qualified to determine your self-worth (particularly if the boy is a creep). The only one who should be doing that is you.

Classmates and Other "Just Friends"

If you think that being a girl limits you to only having female friends, think again. Just because boys and girls are different, just because there are some guys you want to smooch and others you want to smack, doesn't mean there isn't a boy or two out there who could actually be an amazing pal.

It is possible to have a civil, friendly relationship with boys. After all, they are just people. Friendships with boys can be a great way to get a better understanding of the guy experience. And even if you're never able to figure out what they could possibly like about professional wrestling, you might find that a guy pal can lead you to some clues about why boys do what they do. You may find that you have way more in common than you ever would have thought.

Sometimes, of course, things get

complicated. Imagine if you will the following situation. You love having Cody for your science lab partner because not only does he not mind measuring out compounds while you do the math equations, but he has a never-ending supply of jokes that keep you nearly rolling down the aisle with laughter. There's just one tiny problem: You are happy in the friend zone, but Cody wants to take you to the school dance. Basically, you're the crush who wants to be "just friends."

Though there is no one formula, here's a simplified Do-and-Don't list to ponder:

DO
- *Try to understand his feelings.*
- *Be honest with him about your feelings.*

DON'T
- *Ridicule or pity him for his feelings.*
- *Tell him things that you don't really mean.*

Yes, it's that simple. Treat him the way you would like to be treated in the same situation.

"When he asked me out on a date, I told him that I'd rather keep it in the classroom," Tyra explains about a boy who likes her. "I like him, too, but I would rather we were just friends."

Be Kind

Don't forget: Boys are people too, believe it or not. They can be as uncertain, nervous, and insecure about girls as girls can be about them. Consideration and kindness can go a long way—for boys *and* girls.

"We're friends, but I think he wants more. I'm thinking about it," Teresa says about a boy she might be interested in. "He's cute, and he's intelligent, and he's kind. But it has to be my decision. Dating has to be something that would be right for both of us."

"I think about kissing him, but I'm worried about losing his friendship," Charlene says about an issue that every girl faces sooner or later.

It might seem easier to tell him creamy white lies or what you think he wants to hear, but you won't be sparing anyone's feelings—his or yours—by doing so. In the long run, the truth is easier. In the same situation, if you really think about it, wouldn't you want him to tell you the truth?

Girl Power!

Until the 1970s, girls were taught to believe that a woman's place in the world was in the home. Today a large number of American girls will go to college and work outside the home. Women are facing the world with more choices and opportunities than ever before. Even so, women still encounter a multitude of problems that result from discrimination (unfair treatment due to their sex). Fighting for equal pay for equal work, putting an end to domestic violence, and making education and health care more accessible are all struggles that younger generations of women will have to take up.

In the meantime, you can make your world a better place by developing healthy and respectful relationships with your peers, and that includes guys. In your life there will be guys who are your

mega-crushes, your classmate pals, and total creeps. In the end they're all people, just like you, but you always will be the one calling your own shots. You can make it to adulthood with the self-confidence to face the challenges ahead if you trust your instincts, stay informed, and believe in yourself.

Sound too simple? Then consider the Girls' Bill of Rights. It was created by Girls Incorporated, the national youth organization dedicated to helping every girl become strong, smart, and bold, and preparing them to lead successful, independent, and complete lives.

Girls' Bill of Rights

•*Girls have a right to be themselves—people first and females second—and to resist pressure to behave in sex-stereotyped ways.*

•*Girls have a right to express themselves with originality and enthusiasm.*

• *Girls have a right to take risks, to strive freely, and to take pride in success.*

• *Girls have a right to accept and enjoy the bodies they were born with and not to feel pressured to compromise their health in order to satisfy the dictates of an "ideal" physical image.*

• *Girls have a right to be free of vulnerability and self-doubt and to develop as mentally and emotionally sound individuals.*

• *Girls have a right to prepare for interesting work and economic independence.*

adolescence   The time of life between puberty and maturity.

condom   A sheath worn by men over the penis to prevent conception or the transmission of disease. Aside from abstinence, condoms are considered the best protection against AIDS and other STDs.

contraceptive   A device, substance, or method that is used to prevent a woman from getting pregnant.

homosexuality   Sexual attraction to a member or members of the same sex, or the behavior that results from such attraction.

hormone   Any of several substances produced by living cells that circulate through the body of a living organism and act to produce a specific effect in other cells. Examples of human hormones include epinephrine (adrenaline), estrogen, and testosterone.

masturbation   Sexual self-stimulation.

menstruation   Monthly discharge of blood, tissue, and secretions from the uterus that occurs when a woman is sexually mature.

period   Menstruation.

puberty   The state of physical development when it is first possible to bear or conceive children.

pubic hair   Hair that covers the lower part of the abdomen surrounding the external genitals.

sexually transmitted disease (STD)   A disease transmitted by sexual contact between two individuals. Examples of sexually transmitted diseases include AIDS, chlamydia, and syphilis.

stereotype   A generalized image of the characteristics of a specific group of people (for example, African Americans, women, Germans, etc.) that is then thought to apply to all individuals of that group.

It's a Girl's World:
helpful info

Web Sites

There are a whole lot of things a girl can do on-line. If you have access to the Internet, either at school or at home, you can visit these great, girl-friendly sites:

http://girlspace.com
An informative site—with Q & A—about puberty and specifically menstruation, developed by Kotex.

http://www.chickclick.com
Girls galore! Sites for all sights and points of view.

http://www.girlpower.com
Encourages and motivates the coming-of-age female, specifically through writing.

http://www.girlsinc.org
The official Web site for the national organization Girls Incorporated (ages six to eighteen).

http://www.girlson.com
The word according to Girl! Girls on Film, Girls on Books, Girls on Girls, and more.

http://www.gURL.com
Humorous yet realistic look at sex, emotions, body image, relationships, and more. Also, you can set up a free e-mail address through this site!

http://www.teenspeak.com
Fashion, music, movies, relationships, boys, sex, you name it!

Reach Out
Association for Women in Science
1200 New York Avenue NW, Suite 650
Washington, DC 20005
(800) 886-2947
Web site: http://www.awis.org

4-H Council
7100 Connecticut Avenue
Chevy Chase, MD 20815
(301) 961-2840
Web site: http://www.fourhcouncil.edu

Girl Scouts of America
420 Fifth Avenue
New York, NY 10018-2798
(212) 852-8000

Girls Incorporated
120 Wall Street, 3rd Floor
New York, NY 10005
(212) 509-2000
fax: (212) 509-8708

International Center for Research on Women
1717 Massachusetts Avenue NW
Washington, DC 20036
(202) 797-0007
Web site: http://www.icrw.org

Take Our Daughters to Work Day
Ms. Foundation for Women
120 Wall Street, 33rd Floor
New York, NY 10005
(800) 676-7780
Web site: http://www.ms.foundation.org

By the Book: *further reading*

Blume, Judy. *Are You There God? It's Me, Margaret.* New York: Dell, 1970.

Carlip, Hillary. *Girl Power: Young Women Speak Out.* New York: Warner Books, 1995.

Gravelle, Karen, and Jennifer and Debbie Palen. *The Period Book: Everything You Don't Want to Ask (but Need to Know).* New York: Walker, 1996.

Harlan, Judith, and Debbie Palen. *Girl Talk: Staying Strong, Feeling Good, Sticking Together.* New York: Walker, 1997.

Jukes, Mavis. *It's a Girl Thing: How to Stay Healthy, Safe, and in Charge.* New York: Knopf, 1996.

Madaras, Lynda. *What's Happening to My Body? A Book for Girls: A Growing Up Guide for Parents and Daughters.* New York: Newmarket, 1987.

McCoy, Kathy, and Charles Wibbelsman. *Life Happens: A Teenager's Guide to Friends, Failure, Sexuality, Love, Rejection, Addiction, Peer Pressure, Families, Loss, Depression, Change, and Other Challenges of Living.* New York: Perigee, 1996.

Ms. Foundation for Women. *Girls Seen and Heard: 52 Life Lessons for Our Daughters.* New York: Penguin, 1998.

Wolf, Linda, and K. Wind Hughes. *Daughters of the Moon, Sisters of the Sun: Young Women and Mentors on the Transition to Womanhood.* Gabriola Island, BC: New Society, 1997.

Index

Credits

About the Author
Elizabeth Frankenberger is a freelance writer in New York City, where she also works for a literary agency.

Photo Credits
Cover photo copyright © NavaSwan, p. 6, Everett collection; pp. 9, 13, 20, 27, 29, 37, 40 by Scott Bauer; p. 15 by Thaddeus Hardin.

Series Design
Laura Murawski

Layout
Oliver Rosenberg